Healing Flows

Ambi Shantay

FOREWORD BY JASON SCALES

"Lord my God, I called to you for help, and you healed me."

Psalm 30:2 (NIV)

Deborah,

Keep being the
obedient one. I
would need to see God
more thru you!

Blessings,

Acknowledgements

All Honor and Praises to my Lord and Savior, my Daddy, for trusting me with an assignment such as this. You challenged me with this, Lord. I pray you are pleased.

Thank you to my family and extended family, my "village" for believing in me and holding me accountable during this journey. Thank you for praying for me when I could not pray for myself. I don't have to list any names. You all know who you are. Know that I felt EVERY prayer!

To my shepherds, my pastor and first lady, Pastor Jason and Lady Barbara Scales, thank you for covering me for such a time as this. Thank you for your obedience. Your teachings have forever changed me.

To the woman that gave me life, my mother JoAnn, I could never thank you enough for how you have stuck with me on this journey of discovery. I love you forever!

To my husband, Jurry, you have shown me love no less than unconditional. I thank you for being the man that Christ created you to be for Jahzyah and me. I thank God for you and your life. It hasn't always been easy for us, but I guarantee you, the best is YET to come. I love you!

Lastly, I dedicate this book to the little seven pound, two-ounce bundle of joy who changed my life forever two years ago, my Jahzyah Joelle.

About the Author

Ambi S. Smith is a wife, mother, and a minister. Her mission is to touch and heal the hearts of women who are facing the difficulties that often accompany motherhood.

The Gallatin, Tennessee native obtained her BA in Corporate and Organizational Communication in 2005 from Western Kentucky University and her MBA with a Human Resources emphasis from the University of Phoenix in 2008. In 2011, Smith accepted her calling as a minister. A year later, established the 501 (c)(3) non-profit organization, Sisters in the Name of Christ, Inc. The organization caters to disadvantaged women in the Middle Tennessee area and serves as a local women's ministry. While "author" was not a part of her many titles, Ambi was inspired to share the obstacles she faced on her journey to motherhood through this therapeutic and personal memoir.

Ambi resides in Murfreesboro, Tennessee with her husband, Jurry Smith, and their two-year-old daughter, Jahzyah Joelle.

Contents

Foreword

I am so excited to see more material being released on healing. Faith is like a muscle. The more you use it and intentionally build it, the stronger it becomes. I believe this book will be an excellent tool to build your faith muscle as it pertains to healing. Once you read Ambi's story and insight on healing, you will be inspired to pursue healing in every area of your life.

Healing was made available to every believer through the death of Jesus on the cross. I believe, according to Isaiah 53:4-5, that Jesus not only took our sins upon Himself on the cross, but HE also took all physical, mental, and spiritual sickness and disease!

Isaiah 53:4-5 says, "Surely, he took up our pain and bore our suffering, yet we considered him punished by God, stricken by him, and afflicted. But he was pierced for our transgressions, he was crushed for our iniquities; the punishment that brought us peace was on him, and by his wounds we are healed."

I believe healing can happen in various ways. Someone can get hands laid on them and be healed, but a person can also be healed through getting the Word of God inside of them and trusting the Word of God to be medicine to their flesh. The world *health* in the scripture below can also be translated to *medicine*. I believe you can read, meditate, and speak the Word of God over your life like you would take a regimen of medicine and see the results manifest in your body.

Proverbs 4: 20-22 says, "My son, pay attention to what I say; turn your ear to my words. Do not let them out of your sight, keep them within your heart; for they are life to those who find them and health to one's whole body."

My prayer is that through reading this book, you begin to pursue God for yourself and discover what His Word says to you about healing and be inspired to pursue healing in every area of your life. Healing is for every Child of God!

Pastor Jason Scales

Believers Faith Fellowship

Introduction

I f you are reading this book, it is my prayer that God meets your every need and desire according to His will. I know what it's like to want something so bad and to work for something so hard –yet not see the fruit of your labor. On the other hand, I also know what it's like to put your trust in God completely and submit your will to His own, for it is then when you truly begin to see a manifestation take place in your life. I wrote "Healing Flows" as a direct assignment from my Heavenly Father. Its intent is multi-purposed. My primary purpose was to initially show love and compassion to my sisters who are awaiting the blessing of motherhood. I cannot say that every woman will bring forth life from her womb- that may not be God's will. However, if you submit your will to the will of the Lord, He will give you double for your trouble. I have been there, trust me. On the other hand, it could be something entirely different that you are trusting God for, but the faith walk is the same.

As I began writing, I found myself becoming more and more transparent. I found myself sharing thoughts and emotions that I haven't shared with anyone else. The more I shared, the more I realized that my Daddy tricked me! I was writing these books to help my sisters around the world heal. In return, God was healing me of things I refused to confront. To whom much is given, much is required. God has already shown me my future and what lies ahead. There's no way I could fully walk in the power and authority given to me if I didn't allow myself the freedom to stretch, take inventory of both who I was and who I was not in Christ.

Throughout the pages of this book, I open my heart to you. My deepest struggles have now become my greatest testimonies. I encourage you to seek the Lord for yourself during this time and allow him to be your compass on this journey. Jeremiah 29:13, KJV states, "And ye shall seek me, and find me, when ye shall search for me with all your heart. "After reading this book, you will have a greater understanding of my journey to motherhood and how my faith activated God's power to work in my favor. You will also understand how God had to take me through a pruning process to help me understand who I truly was in Him and all that He desired for me.

My Sister,

Whatever you are standing in need of as you are preparing to read this book, I want to encourage you to tap into the power of our God who has unlimited resources, a God whose well never runs dry. My prayer is that you will not be the same woman once you read this book. I pray that something resonates in your heart and in your spirit that evokes transformation. Most importantly, I hope it heals your wounds. I believe Christ is saying to you just as He said in Matthew 9:29 NIV, "According to your faith let it be done to you."

With Sisterly Love,

Ambi

Chapter One

"I will not violate my covenant or alter what my lips have uttered."

Psalm 89:34 (NIV)

Many of you reading this probably grew up in the church like myself, and you've been doing this thing called "religion" for a while. You know the Word and how to pray. I bet you even know how to scream, shout, and as my husband calls it "pick em'up, put 'em down." Church, in general, taught me much of what I know.

I learned how to let go of self and praise God by sitting in the pews and watching the senior choir and praise team. I learned how to develop a close relationship with God by attending Bible study. It was there I learned how to study the Word and apply it to my situations. Once I learned those things, my worship became more sentimental, prayers became more personal, and my thirst and hunger for the Lord grew. I longed to be in His presence. I knew that there was nothing the Lord could not do. He's everything, He goes everywhere, and He sees everything. He's my Daddy, and He knows me better than I know myself.

What happens when it seems like the Lord isn't near anymore? What do you pray when you're tired of praying? How do you smile when you feel like crying? How can you be everything to everyone while a piece of your heart breaks every day?

The date was May 18, 2014. I remember the weekend because I had some of the teen girls that I mentored at my house. Pastor Jason had an evening service that I was dying to go to. What was ironic about this service was the fact that we don't typically have evening services, and this particular service was just for healing. I didn't know what to expect, but Pastor instructed us to come back if there was any healing we were standing in need of. The girls didn't want to go back to church, so I went by myself. While I wanted to stay at my house and spend the last few hours with my guests, my spirit pushed me to go.

At the time, my husband and I were relatively new members. I didn't know too many people at church, so no one knew my issues. We had been trying to conceive for several months. While I hadn't had any menstrual cycles, I hadn't become pregnant either. My OB/GYN suggested that we try to conceive on our own for a complete year before attempting fertility methods. My doctor, however, didn't know I was already dealing with uncertainty because of how strong endometriosis runs in my family. Also, a prophet asked to pray over my womb some years back confirming what I always had feared – becoming pregnant would be complicated.

So, here I am at this healing service pleading my case to the Lord. God was the only one who knew what my husband and I were going through. We chose not to confide in anyone, not even our parents. The enemy will use some of your closest friends and family to discourage you. I cannot count how many times we heard, "When are the babies coming?" or "I'm not getting any younger. I need someone to spoil." While people's intentions were good and pure, they had no idea that we suffered every time those questions were asked. Must I mention each negative pregnancy test? At one point, I thought I was alone in this journey and that my husband didn't care whether we had a child or not. These thoughts circled in my head until he was at home one day when I took a test. I will never forget the hurt in his eyes or the emotions shared as we sat in the bathroom.

I began thinking back over all those things as I stood in line for prayer. I only remember two words that were prophesied over me when Pastor finally got to me – CRAZY FAITH. He told me that I had "crazy faith," but I was standing in my way. In a blink of an eye, I went down to the ground. My knees buckled, and I went limp. When I got back on my feet, something about me felt different. My spirit felt renewed. I felt like a new creature. When you become new in Christ, everything about you has to change. God deals with us as we are.

He isn't concerned with the past. For me to become a new creature, I would have to put in work!

For days, I replayed those words in my head – crazy faith. I knew faith was a spiritual gift that I possessed, but I honestly didn't know how long I could continue to be faithful. I was being tested, however, I knew if I wanted different results, I had to do things differently. For starters, I had to learn how to shift my thinking and my prayers when I petitioned the Lord. Healing was granted to us over 2000 years ago. The Word tells us we are healed by His stripes; but to be healed, there has to be a condition. I had to admit to myself and profess to the Lord that my body needed His healing touch. A major issue I have with Christians today is that we don't like to admit when there is a problem. For God to heal, we must believe that He CAN heal. A lot of people are in church every Sunday, yet they don't believe in the power of God. I learned this through my mother's healing testimony. Our God does not respond to our conditions; He responds to our faith. I had been praying and praying, yet I wasn't seeing anything moving on my behalf because I wasn't aligning my faith with what I was asking God to do. Pastor Jason always tells us, "You'll get no more from God than what you put in."

I studied my notes from church, and I dived into the Word. If I was to believe in God's power to heal, I first had to know what His Word said about healing, and I had to believe in that Word. I found some scriptures to meditate on and reminded God of His Word when I prayed. I held him to His Word.

Not only do we have to change the way we pray, but we also must have the faith to receive our healing. Let me try and break it down for you. When I say change your prayers, I am referring to the things you are asking God to do. Instead of going to God with the same generic prayer, "Lord, please heal my body if it's in your will" or however you've been praying, be specific. If you know the Lord, you don't have to ask Him. **We have a right to be healed!** The Lord gave us that right, but Jesus isn't healing anyone who does not want to be healed. I go into more details about my prayers in the next chapter, but just know that I prayed a prayer that reflected how I was healed. Even if God didn't heal me that day, month, or even that year, I knew I was healed regardless of how slow the healing process may be. My desire was just to be healed. My sister, be careful of what you pray for! Say what you mean and mean what you say. Often, we find ourselves praying prayers that we don't mean. Be conscious of the words you allow to flow both in your ears and out of your mouth.

The following week, my husband and I went to Bible study. After it was over, I was approached by one of our intercessors. She didn't know anything about me at the time, so she asked if we could talk. To my surprise, she asked me if we wanted to have children. She then explained that she hadn't been obedient to the Lord because that Sunday when I went up for healing, the Lord showed her things concerning me, and she neglected to tell me. She began to say to me that the Lord had shown her a visual of the female anatomy and how everything is aligned. If one body part or organ isn't in alignment, it throws off the entire body. The Lord revealed to her that my body wasn't aligned right just yet. It didn't look like the picture that is portrayed, but by faith and declaration, it would be. I am reminded of 1 Corinthians 12: 22-26 NRV, "...The parts of the body that seem to be weaker are the ones that we can't do without. The parts that we think are less important we treat with special honor. The private parts aren't shown. But they are treated with special care. The parts that can be shown don't need special care. But God has put together all the parts of the body. And he has given more honor to the parts that didn't have any. In that way, the parts of the body will not take sides. All of them will take care of one another. If one part suffers, every part suffers with it. If one part is honored, every part shares in its joy."

Now, I do not suggest you listen to everything that goes in your ear nor do I advise you to tell everyone about your problems. However, I do suggest that when you are praying and believing God to move on your behalf, you should ask him to speak to you so clearly in a manner that you cannot deny it. God can speak to us in so many ways. He can speak to us through the pages of a book, message, through a dream or vision, or in my case, through prophecy. If you are still long enough, you can "hear" from God yourself. Although it won't be face to face conversation, your answer will still be just as clear. However, if you are already in a state of frustration or dealing with cloudy vision, asking God to speak to you directly may not be beneficial to you.

If I obeyed God's word and moved according to His plan (because He always gives us a plan), then I would receive my healing, and the Lord's promise would be fulfilled.

My sister, what is your promise? If you haven't received your promise yet, how are you expecting the Lord to move on your behalf?

Chapter Two

"For I know the plans I have for you," declares the Lord, "plans to prosper you and not to harm you, plans to give you hope and a future."

Jeremiah 29:11 (NIV)

When the Lord gives you a promise, it's always followed by a sign and a plan. If you are ever pondering on a promise from the Lord, consider this- did you receive a plan and a sign?

In the book of Genesis, God enters into covenant with Noah after seeing all the wickedness that prevailed in the world. He assures Noah that he will never destroy the world by flood again (promise). God instructs Noah to build an ark for him and his family to survive as God was making plans to destroy the world by flood (plan). "I have set my rainbow in the cloud, and it is the sign of the covenant between me and the earth," Genesis 9:13 NIV.

God also makes another covenant in the book of Genesis, and this is one of my favorite examples of faith. In Genesis 12, God enters into covenant with Abraham and promises to make him the father of many nations and bless his descendants. Those who are familiar with this story know that Abraham and Sarah were both very old and nowhere near childbearing age. God made Abraham's name great among the nations, and the Lord did indeed bless them with a child.

Okay, so I have shared my promise, but it means nothing without the activation of my faith. What did the Lord instruct me to do? He told me to print off a copy of the female anatomy and pray over it daily and speak life over my situation. Remember, He said previously that I have crazy faith, and now He is telling me to activate it! Someone reading this may not know the power of prayer. This may be your first walk with God, and you may not know how to make a declaration of faith. You may not even know what to pray. I cannot give you the words to pray because this is your faith walk, but I will tell you some of the declarations I made. I will also include some scriptures throughout the book that ministered to me during this time.

I was clueless as to what to pray for because I didn't know what was wrong with my body. I began to pray generic prayers until I received further clarification from the Lord. The more the Lord revealed, the more defined my prayers were. Be specific! Oh, and I wasn't asking, I was proclaiming! In Romans 4:17, God tells us to speak those things that are not as though they were. So, I thanked God for regulating all levels in my body. I commanded every organ to be in proper alignment and function as it should. I thanked God for complete and total healing. I declared that my body would be made whole and I will carry a child full-term. When you are walking by faith, there can be no room for doubt. You can't pray and still worry. So, when I was praying to God, I didn't pray out of fear or doubt. I prayed with the authority that has been given to me through the blood of Jesus. Mark 11:24 (NIV) says, "Therefore I tell you, whatever you ask for in prayer, believe that you have received it, and it will be yours." This scripture tells us that we must believe that when we ask, God has already delivered! We are such impatient people. We want what we want –when we want it. In the Kingdom of God, it doesn't work like that. Sorry, it just doesn't. "For my thoughts are not your thoughts, neither are your ways my ways, declares the Lord. As the heavens are higher than the earth, so are my ways higher than your ways and my thought than your thoughts", Isaiah 55:8-9 NIV.

It was my personal decision not to seek a physician until all options were exhausted because I knew God to be Jehovah Rapha. He is the best physician. I watched him heal my mom and deliver her from a brain aneurysm a few years prior. So, I knew what God could do, and I knew and believed that if He could do that for my mom, then He could surely do it for me too. My mom was on a hospital floor where most people didn't make it out in their right minds. She came out without a trace of an injury, so why would I doubt him? As I am typing this, God is bringing to my remembrance the lyrics of Tye Tribbett's song, "Same God" they state:

"If He did it before, He'd do it again

Same God right now, Same God back then."

The more I prayed, the more I felt my faith being restored. The feelings of hopelessness and failure were gone, and my faith was connecting to my power source. I started believing the things I was praying for. That's the power of prayer! I had to stay in the Word during this time because I had to hide his words in my heart. It had to be a reminder when my flesh would arise and allow doubt to creep in. I was acutely aware that Satan was on the prowl and knew how sensitive of a matter this was. I had to keep on my armor.

I thank God for the piercing pain that struck near my shoulder almost three years ago. It led me to this small chiropractic office in Murfreesboro, Tennessee that greeted me with my name on the wall and I knew I was led there for a reason. To top it off, my chiropractor is a very spiritual man and would often time pray with me during a visit. During my first visit, he sat down with me and said, "I don't know what led you here to this office, but I do believe that God sent you here. Whatever the reason may be, I'm going to fulfill his purpose."

I decided to ask my chiropractor during a visit to show me which nerves in my body were pinched and what each nerve had access to. It's a known fact that every nerve affects multiple parts of the body, not just the area that is hurting. He showed me using the human anatomy as my visual and what he showed me sent me out of the office in tears. The nerve that had been bothering me in my neck was connected to my cervix, how ironic?

Do you know what's even more ironic? God had already begun working on my body before I even knew there was an issue. That's what we call "provision." God was already at work on your situation way before you even knew the problem. In all thy ways, God is higher. He is always at work in our lives.

God's Word instructs us that faith comes by hearing. Our hearing originates from the Word. If you lack the faith needed, which is only just a tiny portion, I encourage you to get planted in your life manual, your Bible. Find scriptures that are relatable and minister to you. Personalize them. Make them your own. On the next few pages, I share with you some of my favorite healing scriptures that helped me during my journey. I am also leaving you space to share your thoughts and testimonies, about what each verse means to you. Feel free to use these pages as a moment of honesty and introspection.

aith & Healing Scriptures

James 1:6

_____

_____

_____

_____

_____

_____

Luke 18:27

_____

_____

_____

_____

_____

_____

Mark 11:24

_____

_____

_____

_____

_____

_____

_____

Mark 5:34

Matthew 8:2-3

Hebrews 11:6

Matthew 8:17

Joshua 1:9

Isaiah 41:10

Matthew 11:28

Psalm 109:19-21

Isaiah 53:5

James 5:16

Psalm 89:34

Matthew 17:20

Luke 1:37

2 Corinthians 5:7

Proverbs 3:5-6

Psalm 46:10

Chapter Three

"Blessed is she who has believed that the Lord would fulfill
his promises to her!"

Luke 1:45 (NIV)

During the next few months, my husband and I
began getting more active in the church. We
began sitting down with couples who had more
experience than us, and we were fortunate enough to
bond with quite a few. However, this one particular
couple left an impression on us. Before we parted ways
one particular evening, I recall them asking us if there
was anything they could pray for on our behalf. Finally,
someone we could confide in! They didn't know enough
about us to make us feel bad about not being able to
conceive, yet their relationship with Christ was evident.
I knew if they said they would be praying for us, they
really would be praying for us. When we expressed to
them what we had been standing in agreement on, they
began to tell us their difficulty conceiving and giving us
some prayer strategies that worked for them. These
strategies blew my mind! My mouth was wide open after
hearing their testimony. Their declarations of faith
worked! We tried some of their strategies for a few
weeks, but in my spirit, the Lord was telling me, "I have
already told you what to do," so, I remained obedient to
what the Lord had instructed me to do.

For two months, I was obedient in my praying, and I was placing my trust in Him, but the months were rolling by, and I was thinking about how my deadline to conceive was approaching. That was my first mistake. I was trusting God on my terms. We can't choose the conditions under which we will place our trust in the Lord. It's either all or nothing.

I started speaking with some of my friends and sorority sisters who were trying to conceive as well. We were comparing our doctor visits. They seemed to know a lot more than I did from speaking with their doctor, so it was a relief to hear what they were going through and the different opinions of each physician. After talking to a few people, I decided to get a second opinion, so I contacted a physician in Nashville to run some tests. Note- this was something that I was saving as a last resort. I was about to count God out. By contacting a doctor, my actions were saying that my problem was too big for God. I should have been speaking to my problem.

The day before I was scheduled to go to Nashville, August 26, I woke up extremely sick. I was so sick that I was miserable. I was thinking, "This can't be my life." I had this big appointment at one of the best women's centers in Nashville the next day, and I couldn't' miss it. I remember my husband calling me wanting to talk, but I kept trying to get off the phone. He was worried about me. The more he worried, the angrier I became. I remember him saying, "You need to take a pregnancy test. You're pregnant." This infuriated me because I had taken so many pregnancy tests and they were all saying the same thing, NEGATIVE! Even when I felt like my body was changing, the tests never confirmed that I was pregnant. They didn't even show a small sign of being pregnant. I remember hanging up the phone and being frustrated, but I still went downstairs and pulled a pregnancy test from the "collection." Yes, I said "collection." I was clearing every shelf in the store. It was too embarrassing going multiple times, but more than embarrassing, it was heartbreaking. Anyway, I took a test at the request of my husband and just like that; I was pregnant! These same tests that I had been taking every week, every other day, for several months were now showing that I was pregnant!

While I was both overjoyed and in disbelief, I had started to become extremely nervous. It took so long for me to become pregnant, I began to question if this pregnancy would even last. All these thoughts ran through my mind, and I had no one but God to confide in. Because both families wanted us to have a child so bad, I didn't want to get their hopes up and make it worse for us to cope with a loss by telling them right away. Besides, no one knew of our struggle anyway. This was something only my husband, and I endured. This was something that I cried myself to sleep for most nights. Now that the victory had been won, I couldn't even rejoice.

When I went to the doctor to confirm my pregnancy, I left the doctor feeling even worse. They knew my struggle. I didn't even get a "congratulations. You're pregnant" like you see in the movies. After taking some lab tests, they confirmed I was pregnant while advising me not to tell anyone because my HCG levels were low and anything could happen. As if this "secret" wasn't already hard to contain, I now had to deal with the thought that I may miscarry.

May I offer you a word of advice, my sister? If it is healing that you desire, please make sure that the physician or medical doctor is supportive of your journey. If I knew then what I know now, I would not have stayed under the care of staff and physicians who were not empathetic of my feelings. It makes a difference. It will eliminate a lot of unnecessary tensions, fears, and high emotions in the long run.

Instead of feeling defeated from the warning given to me at the doctor's office, I remembered what I had been praying, declarations I made, but most importantly, I remembered the promise the Lord made!

I'll never forget the time I attended a ministry meeting at a friend's house for church. As soon as I walked in the kitchen, all the women looked at me and said, "Hold on, you're pregnant. You're carrying that glow!" While I should have been excited, I just burst into tears. They formed a circle around me and each one being a mother began to pray over me and speak life over my situation. I remember my friend, whom I hadn't even told yet, said, "Ambi, the Lord told me to let you know that He did this and you can boast about what He has done. Your pregnancy will last," and it did.

I was referred to a high-risk specialist due to my hypertension. Even though my blood pressure was regulated, at a certain point in my pregnancy, my OB/GYN wouldn't be able to treat me if any problems arose. My baby and I were monitored bi-weekly and closely evaluated. Being referred to the Maternal Fetal specialists was the best thing that could have happened for me. I felt so informed during this trying process. They checked every organ and every limb each visit to ensure that my baby was healthy and not affected by my ailments. Who cared that it meant that I was getting stuck with a needle every week? Nothing could make me complain about the beautiful works of the Lord.

I was sick every day, and I mean SICK. It wasn't morning sickness. I was just downright sick, but knowing that the fetus inside of me was given to me directly from the Lord himself allowed me to press forward. I didn't complain, and I continued to praise God for the work that He had done. Only HE could do something so remarkable inside of me. So, I took it all in stride. Even being as sick as I was, I would do it all again. For me, it was a reminder of God's promise.

My support system was and still is phenomenal. My sister friends would come and cook dinner for me. Church friends would invite my husband and me over for dinner because I couldn't cook because every smell coming from the kitchen irritated me. My family took turns staying with us. That ensured my husband was eating right and laundry was taken care of. The further along I became, the doctors started noticing that my placenta was close to covering my cervix. This is called Placenta Previa. Instead of being induced at approximately 39 weeks due to hypertension, my due date was moved to 37 weeks as a scheduled C-section. I was made aware of the fact that my child could have a low birth weight due to inducing and could be in NICU for an extended amount of time if any organs were not fully developed. God had brought me this far. I was convinced that He would not fail.

Chapter Four

Josiah Joel: The Lord has healed. The Lord is willing.

When I discovered I was having a little girl, I recall sitting in my bedroom one Saturday morning talking to God and praying. I began to ask God to give me a name for her that had great meaning and was symbolic of our journey. Her name should indicate the testimony behind her creation. The only stipulation I had was that I wanted her to have her daddy's initials. One thing that sticks out in my mind is the fact that after I petitioned the Lord, I stayed and waited for Him. I didn't get up. I didn't get on the phone or computer. I stayed there and waited.

Sometimes, we just have to be still (Psalm 46:10). In my stillness, a voice whispered Josiah in my spirit. Had I risen, I wouldn't have been able to receive what the Lord was saying. I remember saying to myself, "That's a boy's name. We aren't doing that." The Lord corrected me and told me to look at the meaning and go outside the box. I remained obedient, and I found its meaning. The dictionary stated the Hebrew meaning was "The Lord has healed." I spent countless hours deciding how I could make the name work for me. I scribbled different names and pronunciations and took them to my husband. Expecting a rebuttal, I cringed at what he would say. He looked at the paper and looked up at me and said, "I like it." She would, after all, have his initials. We decided Jahzyah would be her name. Joelle was a middle name that had already been established as it meant "The Lord is willing." Jahzyah Joelle- The Lord has healed and is willing. Based on that day, I had no idea that those words would be all that I had to stand on in the months to come....

Chapter Five

"Count it all joy, my brothers, when you meet trials of various kinds, for you know that the testing of your faith produces steadfastness."

James 1:2 (ESV)

I f it were up to me, this chapter would not exist, but this is life. My life. During my pregnancy, I experienced a few trials that bent me but didn't break me. I am convinced, even today, the strength of motherhood kicked in during these times. Even though I hadn't given birth yet, I had strength like no other.

In December 2014, my paternal family suffered a great loss. My grandfather, Daddy Harold, went to bed on Christmas night and entered through the gates of Heaven before morning. Receiving the call early that morning felt like a punch in the stomach. I got out of bed, dressed, and before I could grab my keys, my husband was already in the car waiting. That was the quickest and quietest drive home I have ever made. I remember talking to God in the car and reminding Him of what He could do. He could heal him. He just healed me. When I arrived at the hospital, I discovered that He did indeed heal Daddy Harold. It was an eternal healing, and Daddy Harold would hurt no more. I was hurt because I had just gone to see my grandparents a few weeks ago to share the exciting news before we made it public and in a month's time, he was gone. That was the first time loss hit home for me. I am and have been incredibly blessed to have grown up with all of my grandparents along with a great-grandmother. I've cried often wishing God would have spared us a few more months, but God knew best. I was five months pregnant when he passed.

Two months later, I returned home one night from dinner with a friend to find that our home had been invaded. I was seven months pregnant flying out of our home trying to get back in my truck. I usually don't leave the house when my husband is at work, but I only left to get a burger with a friend. When I returned, the back door was kicked all the way in, and it felt like I was still outside standing in my living room. I thank God for friends in the right place at the right time. Some more of our friends moved down the street from us, and I drove there until my husband could make it home and meet the police. They only ended up stealing our bedroom television. I always thought that television was a hindrance anyway, but thank God it was only a television. They bypassed my purse, our laptops and tablets, and even our safe. That's evidence that even though the enemy may be strategic, he isn't the smartest.

While I was scared for my life, I was more concerned that nothing that belonged to our dear baby girl was touched. The thought of someone being in my home uninvited made me livid but had they invaded the sweet innocence of my child. All of these ideas going through my head had me at a loss for words. The enemy stirred me up a little with that incident; I won't lie. I felt violated, and I was no longer comfortable. The peace that surrounded me every night- well, it was wavering. That night, I learned how to operate a pistol. Lord knows I didn't want to use it, but I felt as though I had to protect myself. Then, I remembered Psalm 91. I remembered that Jesus is my refuge and He would fight my battles. I remembered nothing happens that He doesn't allow. So, our door was kicked in, and a television was stolen, but we still had our lives. Psalm 91 got me through long nights. I realized it was just a tactic. I knew who I was and most importantly, I knew whose I was. My God was protecting us.

As if I hadn't already been shaken and stirred enough, we encountered fear once again probably a month later. My husband and I had just had a fun maternity shoot, and we had gone back home to change. We both had places we needed to be, both in two entirely different directions. I was almost at my destination when my husband called me in a panic. He had just been hit on the interstate, and he needed me to come. If you know my husband, you would know that for him to call me to the scene of an accident at least an hour away (while I am about eight months pregnant at this time), then you can imagine it's pretty serious. I was frantic, nervous, but I was trying to remain calm. I was nowhere near home, so it was not the time to lose it! Before I could react, I had family calling me, and even friends of ours passed the accident and called to see if we were involved. Everyone assured me that they would stay with my husband, but the car was totaled. That was the longest ride back home. I wanted to feel so many things, but above all else, I wanted to thank God for sparing my husband's life. Situations don't always work out the way we want them to, but when you know the Lord for yourself, you understand that God allows everything to happen for a reason. We were weeks away from delivery, and now we were reduced to one car. Could anything else happen? I mean we had been through every emotion during our pregnancy. Can the sun come out?

Those negative "woe is me" thoughts faded when my husband walked through our door. I was preparing myself to uplift and encourage him. This was another loss that I was sure he would take personally. We had saved our money so that he could have his dream car. I'm not one for titles or material things, but my husband is a hard worker. He wanted an Infiniti, so I encouraged him to get one. And just like that, it was gone. Totaled. The pictures he sent me and the man standing before me were not in alignment. The way his car was totaled and destroyed, there was no way he should have been walking through that front door without a scar or limp! The picture didn't even show a car. It just looked like molded parts. That night, I praised God in spite of our loss. I could have been a widow and a single mother before our baby was even birthed, but God! In John 16:33 NIV, Jesus reminds us, "In this world you will have trouble. But take heart! I have overcome the world."

Chapter Six

*"So is my word that goes out from my mouth: It will not return
to me empty, but will accomplish what I desire and achieve the
purpose for which I sent it."*

Isaiah 55:11 (NIV)

My estimated due date was May 4, 2015, but I was able to choose the day I would indeed bring forth our miracle during my 37th week. My pregnancy had gone well. By my 37th week, I could no longer walk. It hurt too badly, so I just laid on the couch. It honestly felt like the baby would slip on out if I stood up. I still cannot understand, yet I appreciate, the power we women possess. It is not easy carrying a child for nine months. Despite my pregnancy struggles, I was able to drive the 45 minutes it took to get my mother the Saturday before going into the hospital. Once I returned home, the rest of the weekend was a blur, and I could no longer get around. I had to take my lab tests the evening before my C-section, and I was miserable. Needles and shots had become all too familiar over the course of my pregnancy. When you are pregnant and high risk, you can expect to be poked, touched, and violated beyond the norm. If anything went wrong during my operation, the blood that I was having drawn would save the time of running around trying to transplant blood. Monday morning couldn't come soon enough.

I was scheduled to be induced on Monday, April 13 at 7 a.m. Of course, I would choose the 13th; I'm a Delta! My entire pregnancy I had been able to control my blood pressure, but the day I arrived at the hospital, my blood pressure was at stroke level. I don't recall the numbers, but they were near the 200s. I had a village with me that morning. The family had driven down the night before and stayed with us. That was comforting as it took my mind off of going into the hospital. Other relatives surprised us by meeting us there that morning. Jahzyah's godfather had left and shown up in the room as I was being prepped. We had a photographer to capture our birth story, but after they all prayed over me, I wouldn't see them again for hours.

Because my blood pressure was so high, it threw my procedure off. My OB/GYN informed me of the process before going in, and I was to get a spinal tab before my C-section. If there was a chance I could bleed a lot, which is why I was at the hospital the day before, to have blood drawn days before so that it would already be accessible. These details were all that I was told and these details were all that I needed. I didn't need to check Doctor Google to scare me anymore. In all honesty, I wasn't scared. God had brought me through too much, and the evidence was in the attacks the weeks prior. God was about to deliver the greatest blessing ever.

Unfortunately, things happened beyond my control, and I could no longer get a spinal tab. I was informed that I would have to get an epidural, but in increments, because my blood pressure was rising. That is one shot you do not want to be administered slowly. My goodness!

I never quite felt the numbness that comes with an epidural. I only remember being wheeled into the operating room and thought "surely they aren't about to start. I don't feel anything different." That was the longest trip down to the operating room. I envisioned it to be welcoming and friendly, but to me, it was scary and cold. I was shaking as a result of the epidural, but I was not numb. I had feeling in my body. Maybe I was going numb, but I am convinced that I was not completely numb. What's done is done, and it doesn't matter at this point, but I recall questioning what the staff was doing. That was the last thing I remember as someone injected some medicine into my IV making me unconscious. When I woke up from the surgery, I was back in a delivery room surrounded by friends and family, but my baby wasn't. She was in NICU. From this point on, I don't remember much. I am telling you what I do remember or what I remember being said to me. I look forward to the day when my husband will use the platform given to him to share his story as he is the only eyewitness to what I am about to make you aware of.

After you deliver a baby, you expect to see the bundle that you have grown attached to over the course of your pregnancy. When someone delivers a package to you, you want to see what's in the box, right? When I finally woke up that evening, all I could say was, "Where is my baby?" I was told she needed some oxygen, so they sent her to the NICU, and when I was better, I could see her during visitor hours. Because that didn't sit well with me, and my husband knew that wasn't going to sit well with me, I was given pictures the nursery had taken so I could see my baby. I can't quite put into words how I felt. I came to the hospital to have a baby, and I get a photograph. Nothing was adding up, and I felt like everyone knew something wasn't right except for me. Jahzyah had been healthy the entire time. Why would she be in the NICU? Why can I not see her?

Nothing made sense to me. Here I am looking at pictures of the baby I carried for 37 weeks. I didn't even know what time she was delivered, but the card that they left in my room stated that she was born at 9:50 a.m. From the picture I was shown, we had a beautiful seven pound, two-ounce baby girl with a head full of curly hair. Light skin, thick thighs like her mommy, and the cutest chubby cheeks! I remember smiling when I saw her plump little face because I was specific in the things I had asked for, and the Lord did just what I asked. I couldn't fathom knowing why she was not in the room with me. I couldn't say much being that I was heavily sedated, but I did ask my husband to photograph everything as I was "missing" the most critical hours of Jahzyah's entrance into the world. Was she wondering where her mommy was? Even today, I look at her and become saddened that I couldn't be there for her grand entrance into the world. Even though it was due to circumstances beyond my control, as a mother, the thought of feeling like you can't be there for your child is unbearable.

I was actually in worse shape than Jahzyah. I was hooked up to magnesium, so I was confined to bed for at least 48 hours, not having strength or the ability to do anything for myself. Before that day, I didn't know anything about magnesium other than it being an element we talked about in chemistry class. I had no idea that it would save my life. I developed toxemia when I went into the hospital, and the only thing controlling my blood pressure was the magnesium being pumped into me. Although it was saving my life, it was also draining me. Every day I was asking why my baby was in NICU and not in the room with me. I didn't even realize until days later that I wasn't even in a real room. I was placed back in the labor and delivery room, and those nurses were watching over me because I needed around the clock care. That made sense why my "room" was so great- it wasn't meant to be an overnight room stay. "Helpless" can't even accurately describe my condition. I had a catheter attached to me so, I wasn't even going to the bathroom on my own. What makes it worse is that I didn't even know when I was going to the bathroom. My "promise" God just delivered to me was my motivation. I was determined to do whatever was needed to get well.

It is communicated to any recipient that you will usually be in extreme pain from a C-section, but that wasn't the case for me. I have had surgery on my stomach before, that was pain. For me, this wasn't as bad. Although it was difficult for me to get out of bed, I wanted to walk around. I wanted to go to the bathroom on my own because I knew if I could convince myself that my situation wasn't as bad as it seemed, I would be out of the hospital. More importantly, I just wanted to be with my daughter. I was sending every guest, and there were several, to the NICU upon their visit. I wanted them to give me a full report because, for some reason, the doctors were not telling me anything. Finally, after I had spoken with a doctor who was relatively new, he sensed my anxiety and vowed to get some answers for me. At that moment, my mother decided to drop the bomb on me. She proceeded to tell me that during my C-section, Jahzyah stopped breathing and was rushed to the NICU for observation. They wanted to monitor her and make sure everything was ok with her. I bawled like a baby. Just thinking that my baby had to go through this and I couldn't help her. Questions and accusations flooded my brain, and I needed more answers. My husband walked in the room during my breakdown and knew instantly that I must have known. I asked him why he didn't tell me. He said that he and the staff felt like it would hinder my progression. So, he chose to wait until I was out of the hospital. However, since I knew, he decided to tell us everything. I thought I was ready, but I wasn't, and neither was my mother.

Not only did Jahzyah stop breathing after they took her from my womb, but I did as well. I could see the hurt and anguish in my husband's eyes as he recalled the moment. I am not sure who coded first, but I believe that with as many nurses and doctors that were awaiting me in the operating room, they were more prepared for Jahzyah. When my machine started to indicate no sign of life is when husband said he lost it and started screaming. He was there at my side telling me to wake up. We were supposed to be welcoming our baby girl into the world, but my husband was watching both of his ladies slowly leave. He was told to go with Jahzyah. Hearing him recall how the staff started working on me to bring me back to life, was and still is, too much. I haven't made it to the point where I can recall repeating this story without tears. Even though I lived it, I can't imagine witnessing it. This was something he was dealing with by himself because he didn't tell anyone. However, my mother recalled hearing a code being called over the intercom requesting assistance and the thought of finding out after the fact that it was her daughter, was more than terrifying for her. I just thank God I have a praying mother. I told my family that stayed overnight with us before my delivery that my procedure would only last 45 minutes, then I would be in recovery. My mother said she knew something was wrong when it was hours before she heard anything. We even had a photographer there to capture our birth story. That's how important that day was for us. We didn't want to miss a moment. I didn't want to miss a moment. I was prepared for my husband to have more moments with our daughter after the procedure as he would be the one to go back while they cleaned her up. I was not prepared, however, to stare death in the face. Not once, but twice.

To this day, I still have a video that my husband took of them resuscitating our baby. I watched that video when I woke up over and over. However, due to my mental and physical state, I never realized that my baby was lifeless. I see it now. Her body was pale and purple as the doctors steadily and patiently worked on her.

They were so patient and so hopeful. I look at that video, and I see the hand of God present. I see prayers that were prayed that morning being activated. I see healing flowing.

Everyone told me what to expect when I was pregnant and even when the baby arrives, but no one could have ever prepared me enough for the actual arrival of my baby. No one told me that things could go opposite as planned, especially when your procedure has already been planned and prepped for the unknown. Do you enter into the hospital to bring forth life and face the possibility of losing your own? Unfortunately, it happens. I wish it on no one, not even the worst enemy. How grateful I am that on April 13, 2015, God gave me a second chance to be a better woman, better wife, and a new mom. How symbolic is my testimony? What does this preach to you? That for something new to be birthed, something has to die? My God!

I had Jahzyah Joelle on a Monday. On that Wednesday, my nurse came in the room and bathed me. She told me she was going to start unhooking me from the magnesium and afterward, I was going to meet my daughter. I've never heard such sweet words. It was this day, however, that friends and family were stopping by every hour. If you ever wanted to know what you mean to people, you will find out when you're sick. I was grateful for each person who came by. I must have been in bad shape because people were coming out of the woodwork. They added joy to my sad situation and the gifts and flowers that flooded my room let me know how much I mean to people. I was as equally frustrated this particular day because they were coming between my precious child and me. I had to ask the nursing staff to stop all visitors because I didn't want to be interrupted from getting to that little girl.

My heart skipped a beat when I laid eyes on her for the first time, and she gazed into my eyes as if she was just as captivated with me as I was with her. When I talked to her, those beautiful gray eyes looked into mine as if she understood every word. It could have been the fact that I had what she wanted, milk. When I attempted to breastfeed her for the first time, she jumped towards my body. She knew who her mama was. That moment, I was determined to get better. I still had some recovering to do, but I was determined to get better for her. When I suffered, she suffered too.

The NICU had certain hours for visiting; no one could be back there during shift change. They preferred mothers to come at feeding and bath time so we could tend to our children personally. I wasn't that well yet. While it was my intent to go at each designated time, post-partum side effects were kicking in, and it did not agree with my hypertension. Each day afterward, I was rejected dismissal because something else always arose.

Not only was my blood pressure elevated, but I was also now having anxiety attacks. My clothes would be drenched from multiple hot flashes (and my room was freezing). The nurses constantly had to change my bed sheets because of how much I would sweat. I was expressing these things to my physician, but she was completely disregarding me. It was a male physician who happened to be on call when I had an attack who genuinely told me that what I was experiencing was normal and prescribed some medicine for me to take. What a huge relief it was to find out what I was experiencing was normal. Nights, however, were terrible! If I couldn't sleep, no one could sleep. I was constantly tossing and turning, crying, etc. The nurses asked my husband to get in the bed with me to remind me of my "norm." It didn't work. I'm sharing this with you because no one shared it with me, and I would have never guessed I would have fallen victim to depression. According to the Centers for Disease Control, 11 to 20% of women who give birth each year have symptoms of postpartum depression.

I started feeling defeated, and a dark spirit had come over me. I could feel the coldness in the room. I thought I could see the enemy looking at me when I looked at my husband. The enemy was winning the battle. I began treating my husband as if he was my enemy. I remember sending him home one night because I didn't want to be around him. My hormones were everywhere. I was so mad, yet I was so sad. I was mad because no one could help me and I was sad because I felt all alone. Throughout our marriage, my husband had given me everything I wanted; I never had to ask. He would just pay attention to the things I liked or to the places I would say I wanted to go. He couldn't heal me from this, and he couldn't get me out of the hospital any quicker. The enemy was in my ear telling me he didn't want to. Instead of fighting back with the Word or in prayer, I gave in to the voices. I had no more fight in me. Thank God for a praying mother. My mother moved in silence. I didn't have to say anything because my silence spoke volumes. She knew that I wasn't myself and she felt the same tension in my room. Every night, and even during the day, she would go to the end of my bed and anoint my feet while praying and rubbing my body. Some nights I would just hop up and ask her to wheel me to the NICU. Although I couldn't touch my child, seeing her rest would put my spirit to rest.

I cannot end this chapter without expressing how the power of prayer will move in your situation. If you are dealing with an issue, weakness, illness, or maybe even a "thorn in the flesh," you need someone praying with you and for you. It could be your spiritual covering, spouse, parent, or maybe just someone who has a credible reputation. Not only does prayer change things, but there is strength in numbers. When you are too broken, like me, to pray for yourself, it's imperative to have someone interceding for you and knocking on Heaven's door for your breakthrough. I am blessed to have my mother there the entire praying at my feet. My mother-in-law was calling and praying, but she was also channeling other prayer warriors to be in prayer as well. Both of my grandmothers had someone bring them to see me. My paternal granny came carrying oil. Relatives out of town were calling and praying with me. My pastor and even a former pastor came by and prayed. They each came by at just the right moments. Even friends from church got together, stopped by, and prayed. During a time when I couldn't pray for myself, I had so many people praying for me. The prayers of the righteous truly do availeth much.

On the seventh day, April 20, 2015, I was released from the hospital. Jahzyah had been released two or three days prior from the NICU. She was just in the room with me, waiting for me to get it together. Her pediatrician came in the room and told me Jahzyah had enough. At one week, she already had a little attitude. She didn't want anyone else touching or holding her as she was over in the nursery. Finally, we were headed home. We weren't headed home because I was back to normal, but because I had started showing signs of improvement. The symptoms I was having were all familiar. I knew my blood pressure wasn't going to go back to standard overnight because of the toxemia, but by the seventh day, it was a lot better than it was. So, the staff was hopeful that I would get better over the next few days. I just had to make sure that I was still taking it easy. That meant I couldn't get too excited or too emotional or my blood pressure would skyrocket. When this happened, I was instructed to lay down on my left side in a dark, quiet room. I've never heard of this remedy before, but I promise it worked every time.

The nurses were so good to me. They joked about me being a vet on the floor and how I could teach the new moms class that everyone on the floor had to attend before we were dismissed. One nurse, an older lady from New Orleans, had stopped by just to wish me well. She was very compassionate, and I loved her presence. She must have been a grandmother because she was so gentle and kind. I remember her telling me to think twice before becoming pregnant again. I never forgot that conversation. I know it didn't look good from the natural eye, but she and everyone else failed to realize that God had already accomplished so much on my behalf when things didn't look good. If it is or was His Will for me to have another child, there's nothing any of us can do about it. That was a conversation I wasn't ready to have yet, so I Just said, "Yes Ma'am" and we parted ways. It was far too early for me to even think about having another child or visiting the hospital for an extended stay. I was just ready to go home!

Chapter Seven

"The Lord is close to the brokenhearted and saves those who are crushed in spirit."

Psalm 34:18 (NIV)

M y mother took a leave of absence to stay with us for at least a month, which was nothing short of a blessing. It was unfortunate that a week of her month's stay was spent in my hospital room, but I know she wouldn't have wanted to be anywhere else. My husband went back to work after I was dismissed from the hospital. He joked about how my mother wouldn't let him help with anything anyway, so he may as well go and make us some money. Even with my mother there, I was still experiencing difficulty.

Breastfeeding Jahzyah took so much of my energy. When we were in the hospital, I discovered approximately three days into our visit they were not giving her any formula because they knew that I desired to breastfeed. However, I couldn't feed her while I was on magnesium. It wasn't until they unhooked me from the machine that I was able to pump (unless someone was doing it for me) or even feed her myself. I was under the impression that they would just give her formula, but I was mistaken. I was distraught, but what could I do? I was in no shape or form able to physically get up and feed her. So, I asked them to give my baby some formula. I still credit Jahzyah's appetite to this account. So, because of the supplement during my illness, I chose to continue to supplement with formula even when we were home. Besides, I wasn't producing enough milk to satisfy my child's hunger. She was hungry and because I still didn't feel well and I couldn't devote my time to pumping as frequently as I should have. When I forced myself to take a chance to pump, it became a hassle. Infants should eat every few hours, and every few hours, I felt my pressure rising because she was antsy and irritable. In the state of mind, it was just too much. I didn't understand that my baby was relying on me. All that I could grasp was that I was failing at this thing called motherhood. The one thing that I looked forward to doing, bonding with my daughter, and she was rejecting me also. I felt hopeless. When I went to my OB/GYN for my six-week checkup, I was forced to stop breast feeding. Not only was my blood pressure not looking good, but my doctor knew my mental health wasn't either. Thankfully, I was able to give her the most vital nutrients that she needed in the first few weeks.

There are not enough words in the dictionary to explain how I was feeling. These are things I never shared with anyone. I was in such a dark place that I had no emotions. I take that back. I had emotions; I just stopped caring about them. I was still a little light-headed from my elevated blood pressure. I was extremely frustrated because even though my pain wasn't a hindrance, it seemed like every other thing was. I had started to envy my husband because I watched him go to work, run errands, do whatever he needed to do, and I was just stuck. I began to convince myself that he didn't care about me or what I was going through or feeling. "His world didn't change, mine did," I repeated to myself. I wasn't driving, wasn't leaving the house, and I didn't want to. On top of all the feelings and emotions, I now have been restricted from one of the most intimate moments between a mother and her child. I felt inadequate.

As a mother, I felt that I couldn't give my child the very thing a woman can naturally give their seed. I prepared for motherhood the best way I could. I had a pantry filled with things I would need for breastfeeding and feeding when she could begin to eat other foods. And after one doctor visit, my hopes were crushed. Even though I knew before the doctor visit that this was all too much for my physical health, nothing is more depressing than having someone take that right away from you. This, however, is coming from someone who has a fear of rejection.

Along with the feeling of inadequacy, I also felt betrayed. Did I just tell you this? This has been my biggest kept secret for two years. Why? Because I was ashamed to open my lips and let those words come out of my mouth because in my mind I knew better. Even though I knew better, that didn't change the way I felt during this particular time. I have since asked for forgiveness, but I will admit that I was mad at God. I felt like He and I were better than that. I had been faithful to my callings, doing whatever He asked, giving, etc. I had been through life and death situation before with my mother back in 2007, why must I be used again. I didn't stray away from Christ, but It was hard for me to see Him at work in my life during this time. Most days, I would just sit on the couch and cry, even with people in the room. I could always find an excuse as to why I was crying, but only God knew the real reason.

Well, I thought God only knew. I was recently talking to my mother about this dark moment, and she shared with me how she was concerned about me because she knew I was not myself and she pulled the family aside to warn them. She said that she knew everyone was expecting me to enter into motherhood at a fast pace, organized, independent, and not needing much help tending to my child. My mother said the breastfeeding incident, or my lack of breastfeeding, showed her that I wasn't right. She said, "You have always been superwoman, but when I watched you struggle to tend to your child, I knew this time you needed help." She put a bug in everyone's ear that I needed help. The more support I received, the lonelier I felt. I appreciated and needed the help, but I felt so incapable. I felt like my purpose had gone. My family was now complete, but I felt so incomplete.

I remember this one incident so vividly. I have never intentionally tried to hurt anyone's feelings before in my life. However, I felt so distant and so disconnected to everything going on around me; I just wanted someone to feel as bad and as little as I did. So, when my husband came home one evening, I exploded. I don't remember what I said, but after I said it, I knew immediately that I should not have said it. He didn't have any idea where it came from, wasn't expecting it, and he didn't know how to handle it. He left the house in shock. As soon as I heard the door slam, I could hear a pin drop. Behind the silence, I heard my mother's voice ask me, "Why did you do that?" I sharply replied, "Because I want him to feel what I feel."

I stated earlier that no one ever told me what could go wrong in the delivery room or with a C-section. They didn't tell me the repercussions of post-partum depression either. I always imagined it to be a visible disorder. I thought that you could look at someone and see signs of depression. From what I've seen and heard, women like that were harmful to themselves and their children. That wasn't me. I was so protective of my kid. I couldn't even sleep because I would check her breathing every few minutes. I was so attached to

Jahzyah. I wouldn't dare hurt her, and I wasn't even trying to hurt myself. I wasn't violent, suicidal, and wasn't overly emotional. I was just internally mad, sad, and disgusted. If I were to be by myself, I would think myself angry. I wouldn't do anything once I became angry, I was just mad, and I would have to deal with it until I exploded on my husband or went crying to my mama. That's why I preferred to be surrounded by people. When other people were around, I couldn't focus on the demon that was stirring up these emotions because I wasn't strong enough to confront it. I had a few ministry engagements I had to postpone because I thought I was going to bounce back as I do with every other challenge I face. This time, I was wrong.

I had visitors consistently for at least two months after Jahzyah's birth. My mother stayed a month, my grandmother stayed two weeks, and my in-laws were always stopping by to check on us. Not to mention, our church family was incredibly kind to us. My friends didn't disappoint either. God blessed me with a healthy support system. I like to call them our "village." Even to this day, when we are praying, we praise God for our "village." They held us down even when they didn't know they were doing anything. Just their presence during my journey meant the world. I expected being married with children would scare my friends off, but they showed me true genuine love during a time I needed it most. So, friends, if you're reading this (and I hope you are), thank you for being true. Even in the midst of this mood disorder, I learned a great deal about who was standing with me and who wasn't.

After the "newness" wore off, I began to adjust to my new normal. I didn't know what else to do. I hadn't yet accepted that I was sick, and no one had called me out, so I just adapted to it and learned how to deal with it. I pushed the thoughts to the back of my mind when they came, and I would just deal with it. I didn't realize it was causing me to distance myself from my husband. I didn't see the strain in my marriage until one day, I was driving home, and a message from one of my prophetic friends came through my phone. I hadn't heard from this guy in quite a while. We are friends on social media, but I wasn't posting much because wasn't much going on in my life besides adapting to this new lifestyle. This guy is one of those deep people who you have to prepare yourself before you receive from them. I ignored the message. I had to be home when I read it. I knew from the feeling in my stomach God was about to speak through Him.

When I got home, I looked at the message. He started off by telling me that God was showing him a dark cloud looming over me that represented the spirit of depression. He assured me after that night; it would last no longer. As I was reading it, I heard God telling me to own it so He can take it. I fell to the floor and sobbed. I cried for all the months I had no emotions to release. I called my mother on the phone and when she answered, I just screamed and sobbed. She had no idea what was going on. I released all my emotions over the past few months. I called her because I was too ashamed to call my husband. I had made him my punching bag for too long. Not physically, but emotionally I dumped all my anger and sadness on him, and I felt horrible.

I remember my mother stopping me during my outpour of emotions and told me not to claim depression and pray. I remember our conversation vividly because I remember my response. I said, "Mama, I have to claim this. If I don't claim it, God can't heal it." She got silent. There was an awkward silence, so I continued talking. I told her all I ever hear from the black community in response to a problem or concern is to pray about it. We are taught not to claim illnesses and diseases. The truth of the matter is if we don't claim it, God can't heal it. Jesus tells us to cast our cares on Him. We have to own up to our issues, regardless of how embarrassing they may seem. This doesn't mean we become a walking billboard because nobody has to ever know, but we do have to recognize that we need God's grace to access our healing. In this book, Kingdom Woman, Tony Evans writes, "Religion can be one of the greatest hindrances to faith because it creates dependency on a ritual rather than on the God of the universe who can do all things."

I recently read an article from Black Women's Health about black women and mental health. It mentioned the difficulties in treating black women, particularly for mental health problems. The main reason is that black women tend to minimize the seriousness of their problems. I thought how accurate that statement was, especially in my own life. I had a nurse from my employer calling me periodically during my maternity leave to make sure I was doing okay and making sure I wasn't experiencing PPD. I gave her no evidence of depression during our conversations. Like every other woman, I suppose I didn't want the stigma attached to me of being "weak." Like my mother said, I've always been one to carry an "S" on my chest. I didn't want t to display my vulnerability to this stranger and have her judge me.

I can boldly declare that when I hung up from talking and praying with my mother, I was empty. God removed every impure and imperfect thought from my body. I was gagging, nauseous, and head was pounding, but I couldn't lie down. I had to call my husband and apologize. I treated him awful. Even if I never actually treated him any different, the thoughts in my head were embarrassing enough. He deserved an apology. When I called him, he answered with so much love in his voice.

During the time it took me to calm down before calling him, my mother had already beaten me to it. I don't know what she said to him, but I can imagine she was concerned and wanted to warn him about all the negative stereotypes attached to the word "depression." But guess what? I was already healed. Just. Like. That.

My husband told me that he had just gotten off the phone with my mother.

"I knew you were sick," he said.

"Well, why did you let me be so mean to you?" I asked.

"Because I love you and I knew you been through a lot and had to get it out some way." He replied.

Listening to his explanation made me cry. He was right, I had been through hell, and back it seemed. But to see with my own eyes that my husband chose to love me through it, showed a love that only God could give. I was going to be okay. God was right there with me. He never left me. If anyone left, it was me.

God had been waiting for me. I went all those months suffering in silence, never inviting the Lord into my situations, never actually claiming even to have a situation, but more importantly never did I invite him back into my heart. I was so brokenhearted and wounded from one bad experience with childbirth that I couldn't enjoy the blessing. I had a husband who loved me unconditionally and a beautiful baby girl. Who wouldn't kill to be in my situation? I stopped looking at my husband as the enemy and stopped entertaining the chatter going on in my head. No, my promise didn't exactly happen the way I anticipated. However, it did happen. God did just what He said he was going to do. He didn't tell me that it would be easy. As a matter of fact, in His Word, He tells us that we will have trouble and we will even suffer. He reminds us that He has conquered the world, so there is no situation we face that He cannot overtake. No word from God will ever fail. It will do just what it was sent forth to do.

As this chapter concludes, I leave you with this quote by Tony Evans:

Even when it hurts, God is with you.

Even when it's hard, God can help you.

Even when things seem out of control, God is for you.

Chapter Eight

"Truly I tell you, anyone who will not receive the kingdom of God like a little child will never enter it."

Mark 10:15 (NIV)

Since becoming a mother, I cannot begin to explain how my life has changed. You can have your whole life planned and the direction you want to travel, but when a child comes into your life, your priorities instantly change. No longer is life just about you, but it's about that precious little being that is now a part of you. For the longest, I just wanted to be Jahzyah's mommy.

I didn't want any other responsibilities or obligations, and I didn't care about any other titles attached to my name. I just wanted to enjoy my little family. I fought so hard to get the opportunity just to enjoy life's simple pleasures, and if it were up to me, I would probably still be somewhere with my little family enjoying the goodness of the Lord. To say that I had lost my identity is an understatement. I didn't lose it; I was ready to hand it over. I didn't want it anymore.... But God.

God is so funny! He makes me laugh. I can be pretty sarcastic at times. My family and friends have grown to love and accept that part of me, and I suppose the Lord has too. He pretty much got me together after a period of dealing with my delay, and He gave me an ultimatum.

I laugh at the word "ultimatum" because my husband often jokes that I gave him an ultimatum in marrying me, but I didn't. I suppose since I started becoming complacent with my new little life as a mommy and had stopped seeking new opportunities to minister and empower my sisters in Christ, God started sending opportunities to me. When I would pray over them, God would always remind me that this is what I asked him to do. That was my prayer before I had become pregnant. I wanted more resources and more opportunities to spread His word. My life, however, changed drastically, and I forgot about my assignment.

In all areas of my life, I had been praying for an increase. I wanted an increase in our bank accounts, my property, my ministry, and my gifts. However God blessed me, I would be satisfied. No way could I increase or enlarge my territory operating out of a spirit of disobedience.

While I am so grateful to the Lord for His blessings and all He has done for my family, I have no right to decide I no longer want to serve Him in individual capacities. It is my cross to carry! It is my assignment. The Lord reminded me of the times I asked him to place me in front of the masses and increase my ministry. He told me the day I gave birth to my baby; I gave birth to a "baby" in the spiritual realm, a new healing ministry. I don't have to worry if I can meet the requirements or fulfilling the job, He has already qualified me. While I was enjoying being a mommy, I wasn't fulfilling my end of the bargain. My job was to now go forth like the woman at the well and tell the Kingdom of God about a man named Jesus who could heal, save, and deliver anybody, because he did it for me.

As I began to operate in obedience, the Lord began to reveal Himself in miraculous ways. He showed me that I wasn't robbing myself of time with Jahzyah, but in fact, I was teaching her by example how to serve God in spirit and truth. I started noticing this while she was still an infant, but now that she is a toddler and nearing her second birthday. My desire is that she walks in her mommy's footsteps, she caters to the heart of God's children and allows her light to shine wherever she goes. We are still working on that light shining everywhere she goes, but her love for the Lord is visible. I try not to let her see me too emotional at church because she begins to get frightened, but sometimes, I just can't help but give God praise for simply being who he is. When I do, I let her know I am just thanking God and when she realizes that, she is okay. With that being said, I know I have a worshipper like David in the making.

My relationship with my daughter ministers to me on a regular basis. The love and adoration that she has for me, as her mother, exemplifies how we as God's children should love and adore Christ. As a newborn, babies gravitate to their mothers because they know whatever needs they have, will be supplied by their mother. As mothers, we have a bond that no one can break or emulate for the simple fact that we carried, nourished, and protected our child(ren) for nine months before they were even born. We know them better than anyone.

In retrospect, Christ knew us before we were ever formed. He tells us in Jeremiah 1:5 NIV. "Before I formed you in the womb I knew you before you were born I set you apart." When I would get overwhelmed, God would send me this reminder. Even in the daily tasks, I would do for my family; I would hear God's voice. Our daughter doesn't worry if she is going to eat or whether she will have clothes to wear or diapers on her bottom. She trusts her parents to supply all of her needs. You can see that dependence and confidence in the way those big bright eyes light up when we walk in the room. She knows we have everything she will ever need. Does that sound familiar? If it doesn't, it should. This is how our relationship with Christ should be. We shouldn't worry about what we are going to eat or our plans for tomorrow. We should live every day knowing that God has already supplied our needs for tomorrow. We may not always know how. I don't always know how I am going to pull things off, but I know God has a plan. So, I submit my will to the will of my Father. It isn't easy, however, just like with any collegiate sport or activity, it takes time, practice, and patience.

We are now in the toddler phase. As Jahzyah gets older, I see Christ more and more in her actions. She will be musically inclined; that is a strong trait that runs on my father's side. I prayed that she was gifted in that area. At nine months, she was singing "This little light of mine." At the age of one, it changed to "Jesus wants me for a sunbeam." Now almost nearing the age of two, she has graduated to "I Love You, Lord, Today" and "Let your Living Water Flow." Don't you know that song? You wouldn't if you are not a fan of Jimmy Swaggert. When I tell you baby girl gets into it, she goes into full-blown worship mode! She prays without being asked. She calls out the names of people she wants to pray for. At any given moment, she is liable to call upon the name of Jesus. She recognizes Jesus as all powerful. When she hears His beautiful name, she straightens up. His name convicts! Can we not all strive to be this child-like? She inspires me daily to be better, pray more, worry less, and trust wholeheartedly.

Over the course of this assignment, I found one thing to be true. Because of my dear daughter, I will never be the same. Beyoncé said it best in her interview with Oprah," My daughter introduced me to myself." When speaking with my husband recently about our walk into parenthood, he began to open up and reveal some things that I never heard him say before. My husband is quite a character; he's always joking and making me laugh. This conversation we had was different. It was personal, somber, and real. One thing that I found to be so simple, yet so true, was when he said, "at that moment that we were in the hospital, we grew up." Life changed. I changed. He changed. Priorities changed. Our dreams changed. Our world changed. For the majority of these past two years since our experience, I focused on what happened to me, how I felt, how I suffered. I never considered the impact of those closest to me. I never considered that they might have suffered just as much, but yet in their way. My husband was right. Everyone connected to us grew up because everyone saw how quickly life changes at the blink of an eye. "You don't get these moments back," he said, "You get mad when I constantly tell you I love you, but you can never get that back."

The Lord is placing it on my heart to encourage someone reading this who may be pondering whether or not the time is right to bring forth a child in this world. The minister and mentor in me say as long as you are married, yes, the timing is right. However, the sister in me recognizes that situations happen. There will never be a right time according to our standards. We will never be in the position we want to be in. We will never make the money we want to make. We will never have enough space as we desire. We, as humans, are just never satisfied.

Let me share this briefly as I didn't give you this insight in the beginning. My husband and I made up our minds that when we first got married, we would wait two years to start having children and we only wanted two. I was 28 when we married, and he was 29. I only wanted one pregnancy. We wanted to live our lives first. We traveled to both Jamaica and Hawaii within those two years and took several vacations, just the two of us. We wanted to get it all out of our system, so when we extended our family, it would be our focus. We both recognized that having children is a pretty selfless act. When we were making these plans, we had no other worries. Financially, we were doing well. My husband alone was making six figures. My paychecks were just spending money, and that's what we did. We didn't expect for our careers to change within the next few years, reducing us to half the amount of income we were once accustomed too. We didn't expect for it to take us longer to get pregnant, making me 31 years old when we gave birth. Despite those shifts in the atmosphere, God's will was done. That's what I am trying to convey. God's will is going to be done regardless. Things don't always go as planned in our lives, but it doesn't stop the blessings. A blessing is still a blessing, regardless of how it was received. Despite our many obstacles, beyond a shadow of a doubt, I know that God's timing is perfect.

It is weird how one tiny person comes into the world and turns it upside down. Everything we do is for her. This book is for her. Our businesses are for her. The words "I can't "will not pertain to Jahzyah Joelle. Fear and faith can't coincide. Just as we comfort Jahzyah amidst her little child-like fears and reassure her that we are right there, I hear the Lord more often gently pushing me to go the extra mile. Whenever Jahzyah reaches an obstacle that she is too frightened to tackle, my husband and I whisper in her ear, "I gotcha." When she hears that, she knows she does not need to worry. Those two words change her whole demeanor. My sister, can you hear God whispering those words to you now? He has you in the palm of His hands. Nothing is too hard for him. Just like my dear sweet Jahzyah, a young child, the Lord our Savior wants you to place that same trust and confidence in Him, the author and finisher of your faith.

Final Words from the Author

"Blessed is she who has believed that the Lord would fulfill his promises to her!"

Luke 1:45 (NIV)

We have made it to the end of this assignment. YAYYYY me! This has been such a healing journey for me, and I hope it has been as helpful to you. I look forward to hearing the testimonies and feedback from my sisters in Christ on how this book has helped you and in what area. I have only done as my Father has instructed. I don't know what's next. I don't know how my obedience will manifest, but I do know that in opening up to you, the reader, I have found an unspeakable peace inside my soul. All is well.

This journey has shown me a strength that I never knew existed. My test has created in me a reliance on Christ that cannot be compromised. When you are trusting God and walking by faith ultimately, it requires you to go to a place that you do not know; one that God will reveal as you walk in obedience. The greatest faith any of us could possess is the ability to believe without seeing. In the scripture verse assigned to this chapter from Luke 1:45, God's greatest blessing is given to those who believe Him.

Your healing, breakthrough, and blessings are yours for the asking. Learn to submit your will to the will of our Father and watch Him bless you in ways that you cannot fathom. The enemy seeks to make us feel segregated, as though we are the only ones going through. You're not! We all struggle, suffer, and endure challenges. We just all go through them differently. Some of us look like what we're going through, and some of us do not. My hope is that after reading *Healing Flows*, your mind and heart will be at ease because healing flows from love and compassion. My hope is that your approach and how you view God will change, that you will draw nearer to Him in a way that you have never done before. I hear God saying "Relationships." He desires a relationship with you, sis. Lean on Him. Love on Him. Place your trust in Him, not man. If you have a spiritual problem, you need a spiritual solution. Jesus is the answer.

Healing Flows Prayer

Do you mind if we pray?

Heavenly Father,

I come to you thanking you for this assignment, an assignment that would allow me to minister to the hearts and minds of your daughters all across the world. I pray that something shared through *Healing Flows* resonates in the hearts, minds, and spirit of its readers. I pray that change occurs. I pray people take their relationships with each other as well as with you seriously because life changes at the drop of a dime.

Most importantly, Lord, I pray healing flows from the pages of this book to the reader just as it flowed while writing. Father God, I pray for supernatural healings in the Name of Jesus. I pray for spiritual breakthroughs in the Name of Jesus. I pray pain, sickness, and depression leaves never to return. I pray relationships are mended. I pray "babies" are birthed, both in the natural and in the spiritual realm. I pray for peace that surpasses all understanding for anyone reading this who is at war in their mind. Jesus, you can fix it! I thank you, Lord for family, my family, this reader's family. I pray your riches upon them. I pray that they will not lack. I thank you, Lord, for my dear sweet Jahzyah, who is the greatest gift ever given to Jurry and me. I thank you for trusting us to be her parents, to guide her and mold her, teach and train her to live a life of godliness. I pray for her light that shines in this world of darkness. I thank you that even in the womb she was leaving a mark on this world. Lord, I thank you for people who didn't give up on me.

With that being said, I pray for those who are lost in the world and unable to find their way. I pray for you to build up men and women who are true disciples, leading people to Christ. I thank you, Lord, for the opportunity to minister to your children. I thank you, Lord, for placing this book in places that may not have seen it elsewhere. I thank you, Lord, for opportunities that are arising as a result of Healing Flows. I thank you for seeds sown and for wisdom imparted. I just thank you, Lord, for Jesus. Thank you for your Son who died so that we can live. Thank you, Lord, for your unconditional love. Thank you for your power. Thank you, Heavenly Father, for the Blood.

Now unto Him who can do far more abundantly than all that we ask or think, according to the power of work within us, to Him be the glory, forever and ever. Amen.

Stay Connected

Thank you for purchasing Healing Flows. Ambi would like to connect with you. Below are a few ways you can connect with her.

FACEBOOK Ambi Shantay

INSTAGRAM ambishantay

WEBSITE www.ambishantay.com

EMAIL info@ambishantay.com

Made in the USA
Lexington, KY
08 September 2017